NO LAUGHING MATTER ...

a short tale of death, and
how to recover from it.

Cee Tee Jackson

This book is dedicated to the following:

* My wonderful & beautiful wife, Diane and our two sons Greig & Brett of whom we are so proud.

* PCs Kyle Reid & Aidan Jenner. I am forever indebted.

* All the amazing nurses, surgeons, doctors & auxiliary staff at The Golden Jubilee Hospital, Clydebank and the Royal Alexandra Hospital, Paisley.

* All my family & friends who have provided support to both Diane and myself through such a challenging period.

CONTENTS

PREFACE

Sudden Cardiac Arrests are devastating events. Only 8% survive one that occurs outwith hospital.

The repercussions for victims, family and friends cannot be under-estimated.

Of course, everyone will deal with their situation in a different manner.

This 'short-read' account does not intend to trivialise the life-changing effects of cardiac arrest.

Rather, it is a 100% true account of how I coped with the immediate days and weeks following my own SCA in April 2023.

Colin (Cee Tee) Jackson

*****

Proceeds from the sale of this book will be donated to the following charities:

SUDDEN CARDIAC ARREST UK

SADS UK (Sudden Arrhythmic Death)

INTRODUCTION:

'Don't boast or be thrilled with your achievement, it may not last forever.'

Around 1:45pm on Tuesday 25th April 2023, a conversation with a client led me to proudly claim that in sixteen years of running my own Pet Care / Dog Walking business, I had not missed a single day of work through ill health.

Four and a half hours later, the thrill of my achievement would come to an abrupt and dramatic end.

My life would never be the same.

CHAPTER 1: "PLEASED TO MEET YOU. MY NAME IS DEATH."

It's funny, I'd never really thought about death much, other than it being an inevitable consequence of life; not until I became a fan of Terry Pratchett's series of Discworld fantasy novels, that is.

One character, Death, features regularly either as a focus of the storyline, or by popping in and out of the books with little cameo roles. Now, he **is** funny.

Obviously, from the perspective of a visited character, his appearance can prove a tad worrying. However, his sympathetic appreciation for humanity, coupled with a sardonic wit, provides some degree of succour for the shortly-to-be deceased - and a great deal of mirth for the reader.

Discworld's Death comes across as a congenial chap,

with a wicked and dry sense of humour and a love of cats. He is in many ways, a man after my own heart … though on this occasion he didn't quite get his hands on it.

*****

I like to regard our real-life, Death along those lines; in a cartoon-like fashion. It comforts me to regard him (for he is a 'he') as a helpful soul – one equal partner in a triumvirate completed by his pals, Life and Fate. They each acknowledge the others' existence and work as a team to guide and cajole us mere mortals through our lives.

Together, they are the ethereal equivalent of the Directing Staff (DS) in the television series, 'SAS: Who Dares Wins.'

Like Santa Claus and The Tooth Fairy they're omnipresent; they can be anywhere and everywhere at the one time. Unlike Santa Claus and The Tooth Fairy, they tend to neither leave presents under a tree, nor a shilling under our pillow.

They run a successful business with a tried and tested model perfected over the eons.

Life is a creator; the archetypal influencer and brand agent, generating an astronomical income via his endorsements. Death's contribution comes from a surreptitious cut of the Inheritance Tax excised by the various governments of the world.

Fate has always adopted more of an admin role, keeping meticulous records and preparing the various size of hourglass appropriate to everyone on the planet. He's also responsible for sourcing the sand and calibrating the rate at which it flows from the top bulb to the bottom.

As you can imagine, calculating individual algorithms for each life born on Earth then quickly assembling the correct sized sand-timer is stressful. Fate has always given me the impression of being perpetually harassed.

All of which probably explains his clumsiness on the evening of Tuesday 25th April 2023 when he accidentally bumped into the timer inscribed in a flowing, ornate, Gothic font with the words **Colin Thomas Jackson / 05081958.**

By the time Fate had righted the fallen hourglass and re-apportioned the grains of sand that had errantly spilled into the wrong bulb, Death had arrived in Linwood, Renfrewshire.

With his long, wood-handled scythe placed on the ground beside me, he fumbled around the dark depths of his robe pockets. But before his cold, bony hands could retrieve his business card, the call came through:

"Sorry Death. My bad … you can stand down."

CHAPTER 2:
JUST ANOTHER
DAY.

For as long as I can remember, I've loved sport and exercise. Even as a pre-teen youngster, I'd be organising 440-yard races around our 'block' against other kids from our street. As I grew older, I ran competitively on the track, road and cross country for my local and famous athletics club, Garscube Harriers.

I played football in the Glasgow Amateur League and when a knee injury deprived me of both running and football at the age of twenty-two, I turned to baseball, playing for successful teams in both England and Scotland. Latterly, and to date, I play tennis (not very well, mind) and visit the gym at least twice a week, interspersed with regular Circuits sessions.

At the age of sixty-two, I decided I didn't need

my knees for as long now as in my twenties and took back to running. Though I hadn't worked up the confidence to run competitively, I did have my 5k time down to marginally over twenty-three minutes, which I was quite pleased with considering a forty-year absence from the sport.

On top of that, I've been a professional dog-walker for sixteen years, covering eight to ten miles a day, minimum.

You could say I was reasonably fit.

*****

The Radio 2 'Ten to the Top' music quiz was interrupted by an incoming phone call. I transferred both huskies' leads to one hand - Shadow and Ghost can be trusted to behave.
"Walk easy," I said quietly. They understood. They knew a treat would be forthcoming – huskies are not daft.

I answered the call.

"Can you pick me up from work tonight, please?"
My wife, Diane, usually gets a lift to and from work with one of the doctors from the Health Centre where she works. This evening, though, her friend had a tennis match.

"Of course," I said in a bright and breezy tone, while cursing under my breath having missed a potential ten-point question in the quiz. It had taken longer than it should, but I had eventually come to accept that some things are just best left unsaid. Discretion can at times be the better part of candour.

"Ok – I'll go for a wee run, down Moss Road, then collect you from the petrol station – I need to top up for tomorrow," I said.

"Great, thanks. See you later, bye."

We keep these chats brief. After forty-one years of marriage, its good to withhold some conversation for round the dinner table.

Shadow and Ghost couldn't believe how quick and easy that was.

"We were good boys, right? What biscuits you got today?"

*****

The remainder of the working day was like any other, with the bonus it was dry. And sunny and bright. It isn't always so in the West of Scotland.

I re-discovered an old walk along the River Gryffe in Bridge of Weir with little Aria, a small, black, mixed species rescue dog from Romania. The river was calm, ambling gently in the dappled spring sunshine. Every now and then, tree branches laden with partially and fully opened leaf buds, bowed in deference to the passing flow, trailing the outermost leaves in the refreshing water.

We stopped awhile just a few yards from a watchful heron as it waited patiently for its intended breakfast to swim into view. It remained hungry as we finally moved on.

The day's other three walks passed without notable event, though it was apparent the return of brighter daylight and warmer weather had led to a change in the calls from nesting birds warding off any prospective intruders.

I returned home and spent time working in the garden, before getting ready for my run. With the advent of warmer weather, I decided to forgo my leggings and fluorescent, fleece-lined top. Don't you just love springtime?

I was slightly later than planned on leaving the house. I'd have to shorten my run if I was to be on time to collect Diane. I suppose the other option would have been to just run faster, but I'd played (and won!) my first tennis match of the season the previous evening and my legs were a bit stiff.

I'm not getting any younger, you know.

As I drove to the start point of my run (an out-and-back straight, flat run along a disused country road populated now by rabbits, deer and buzzards) I passed the petrol station at which I said I'd meet Diane.

I may as well fill up now and be done with it, I reasoned. I pulled in.

I wasn't to know, but that just happened to be the best decision of my life.

CHAPTER 3: RUNNING FOR MY LIFE.

I record all my runs on the Strava App. This one was OK; a bit 'meh,' I would term it.

It was only 1.2 miles at 7' 48" pace, so actually a bit on the slow side. I was feeling the previous evening's exertions in my legs, but it was certainly nothing to cause more than twenty to thirty seconds full recovery.

I got in the car and drove the mile and a half to Diane's place of work. I approached from a different direction than I would normally, and having already visited the petrol station, I drove straight into the large carpark that serves both the Health Centre and a row of large stores, including Tesco.

A travelling fairground had been erected over many of the parking spaces, so I drove slowly. I spotted

Diane coming from one of the shops, briefly stopped the car, and she got in.

I slowly moved off again.

And that's it.

Nothing.

Not an enveloping darkness.

Not a blinding light.

Nothing.

*****

"Colin. Look at me. Do you know where you are?"

I felt restricted. I couldn't move. Why was I lying down?

A woman's face came into my vision. I quickly scanned my surroundings.

"In hospital?" I ventured.

"Correct, Colin. Well done. Colin, do you know what month it is? What year is this?"

What kind of dumbass dream is this? I played along.

"May …. 2022"

There was a pause.

"No wait – that's bollocks. It's April. 2023, right?"

I heard laughter. Was that Diane I could hear?

"He's back! He's alright, Diane. He's back with us" I

heard the woman say.

Back? What did the voice mean, 'I was back?' Back from where? From the shops? What was going on?

*****

I have no idea how long passed before my next recollection. Had I blacked out? Had my mind simply shut down in some kind of protective mode?

"Colin, how are you feeling? You're in hospital. Just lie still. Don't move."

The female voice was soft and reassuring. I quickly looked around the room. They weren't Diane's words, but she was sat by me. And my two sons, Greig and Brett. A further glance around and I saw the nurse.

I craned my neck and took in the surroundings. It sure looked like a hospital room. It smelled like a hospital room.

*Wait. This shit just got real. It **is** a hospital room! What's going on?*

Oops! Did I say that out loud?

"Colin, you're in the Royal Alexandra Hospital in Paisley. You collapsed in your car after picking Diane up from work. You're a very lucky man. You have some broken ribs, so watch yourself – don't move any more than you must."

Phew! Broken ribs. Not pleasant, but at least it's nothing serious.

The morphine and whatever other painkillers I'd been administered must have kicked in again.

Soon it would be morning.

CHAPTER 4: DAWN BREAKS – REALITY DAWNS.

"'Morning Colin. How are you feeling? Did you manage some sleep?"

The nurse moved to the window and partially raised the blind to allow some breaking, early morning light into the room. It was around six a.m.

"I ... I, yeah."

I was already in a sitting position, propped up by four pillows at my back. My ribs hurt. They hurt bad, and it was painful to take a deep breath. Five leads connected my chest to a machine that was registering my heart rate and blood pressure and goodness knows what else.

"I know – it's not easy, all hooked up and sleeping in that position, but you'll get used to it. Just be careful when you must get up. Let me know if you need the commode brought in."

Commode? A portable potty? I looked around the room. Once. Twice.

Nope, no sign of it. I must have left my dignity at the front door on the way in.

Slowly, my mind began to replay some of the conversation with Diane from the previous evening. I hadn't been admitted to hospital simply for broken ribs, had I?

"Do you remember picking me up from work?"

"Yes – you'd been in one of the shops."

"But after that?"

"Nothing. I can vaguely recall being asked the date or something and laughing."

"That was when you arrived here at hospital, before being brought up to this room– you were really confused. You were still high on morphine and were being brought back down."

"So, what happened?"

"You drove about fifty yards after I got in the car, then started talking utter gibberish. More than usual. The car stopped but your foot was stuck on the accelerator, revving and revving but going nowhere, thankfully. You began to make some weird gurgling sound. I jumped out the car and tried to pull you out. A young couple were close by and witnessed it all – together we caught the attention of two policemen who happened to be sat in their car close by. They dragged you out and

immediately started CPR. One then ran to Tesco and brought back the public access defibrillator and they used that to bring you back and kept you alive till the paramedics and ambulance arrived. And then you were brought here."

What the ....?!

I pondered the points deduction from my Tesco Clubcard – there goes my new Dolce Gusto Infinissima Black Coffee Machine, I thought.

It all made sense now. The severity of the situation had not dawned the previous evening, probably due to the medication I'd been given. I'd had the comfort of my family being around me, and then I'd slept. What had seemed so surreal, like a weird dream directed by David Lynch, now became so stark.

I truly was lucky to be alive.

CHAPTER 5: TRUST ME, I'M A DOCTOR.

I had spent only two nights previously in hospital. That was over forty years ago, and for a routine exploratory operation on my knee that involved the insertion of one stitch. The only consequence of that minor surgery was being told I had to give up athletics and football.

This , though was a whole new ball game, entirely.

Yet, that first morning, while being cared for in what I naively thought as a 'private room,' I was surprisingly calm.

("It's a 'high dependency' room, you muppet" was Diane's later, succinct correction.)

I consider myself quite pragmatic. I think I'm reasonably good at accepting a situation without too much by way of examination or questioning. I knew I was in the right place, given what I'd been through, and had full faith and trust in those looking after me.

I felt no pain, other than from several ribs that I'd later have confirmed were broken when CPR was being administered. I knew they'd be uncomfortable for a few weeks or so, but they would heal.

(Understatement of the month, that one).

I'd probably be monitored for a couple of days, given some tablets, told to take it easy for a week or two, and be back home for the weekend.

Smoke me a kipper, I'll be back for breakfast.

Not quite.

By eight o'clock that first morning, I'd had a blood sample drawn; blood pressure taken; oxygen levels monitored; temperature checked; ECG (electrocardiogram) recorded, and painkillers administered.

A female doctor arrived, a small entourage in tow.

For the first time since being admitted, I felt a little uneasy.

"Colin, how are you?"

I don't know why she asked – she was going to tell me anyway. I'm reasonably certain had I said "fine and dandy and ready to go home" she would have put have me right.

"Colin, we've noticed some accelerated heart rhythms overnight and again in the past couple of hours."

I conceded I had felt this myself earlier that morning.

"So, what I'd like, is to try this little trick to steady things – could you blow into this syringe for me, please? That most often works."

Of course I couldn't. I could barely breathe in properly let alone out' due to the pain from my ribs.

She suggested a secondary method, but again I couldn't manage, for the same reason.

"Ok Colin. There's nothing to worry about …"

Oh yeah? I know you're only trying to reassure me; keep me calm. But if there's really nothing to worry about, why even tell me 'there's nothing to worry about?' You know what? I'm kind of worried now.

"I'm going to give you this drug intravenously which will, for a few seconds only, greatly accelerate your heartbeat. That will have the effect of re-setting your heart rhythm. Now, although you'll find it difficult to breathe momentarily, I want you to concentrate on taking that breath, and not panicking. Are you Ok with that?"

What do you bloody think?

The words "Of course" accidentally escaped my lips.

I knew this would be one of several hurdles I was going to have deal with. These people had helped save the night before. I reasoned they wouldn't be proposing anything that could easily damage their 'win / loss' average.

I was rigged up with goodness knows how many more cables and asked to relax.

Relax?

OK – here goes.

The drug was injected and almost instantly, my heart rate increased to an alarming level.

"Now breathe in, Colin," the doctor said. Fearing it may be my last, I tried to make it a good one. But I couldn't.

"Keep it going Colin, you're doing great."

Really?

"Almost there … halfway there now. Just a few more seconds … you should feel it ease now. And it's over. Breathe easy, now Colin."

As the doctor said this, I had the weirdest sensation, like pins and needles of my brain. It felt like my face was on fire. Then within seconds, it was over. My heart rate was normal again.

"How was that?" asked the doctor.

"Easy," I lied.

*****

Having been so lucky in avoiding any notable stay

in hospital for over sixty-four years, I thought I'd struggle. I still wasn't allowed to leave my own room, even to go to the toilet or for a wash but given the (almost literally) grave events of the previous twelve hours, I did feel relatively comfortable.

This was in no small part down the nurses, auxiliary staff and doctors of the Cardiology Ward. I can't praise them enough.

It appeared they were working under considerable pressure, simply from a numerical patients / staff ratio. Surroundings were functional, but when compared to some more modern hospitals (it was opened thirty-five years agon in 1988) I would suggest it falls into the 'old school' variety. Shared toilets, for instance, are not my bag – especially when you're on laxatives to counter the binding effect of strong painkillers.

The remainder of Wednesday and Thursday passed comfortably enough, and I quickly adapted to the routine: awakened around 4 am for blood pressure recordings; awakened again around 6 am for a blood sample; 7:30 am was breakfast. 8:30am and it was time for medication, followed by doctors' rounds some time between 9 and 10am.

I was certainly being well looked after, and the care shown was exemplary.

I still wasn't allowed to leave my room though and had to remain plugged in to the heart monitor 24 /7.

Each afternoon throughout my stay, Diane and

Greig would visit. Neither are drivers and though we live only about five miles from the hospital, getting there by public transport is a bit of a logistical nightmare involving three busses and over an hour and a half travelling time.

(Greig was temporarily back living with us until the purchase of his new flat was finalised. It was just too much of a trek for Brett to get to the hospital daily from his home in the far side of Glasgow, so he'd keep in touch via phone/ Messenger.)

It's at times like this you realise what outstandingly good friends you have.

Our close pal, Anne immediately offered to help in whatever way she could; David, her husband drove my abandoned car back to my driveway. Our immediate neighbour, Ian, volunteered to bring Diane to visits. Diane's boss, Rhianne, rallied a group of Ladies from our tennis club (Strathgryffe Tennis & Squash Club) in a WhatsApp Group to form 'Colin's Cabs,' and provided Diane with a list of who'd be available on day-by-day basis to take her to / pick her up from the hospital.

We were both so very touched and grateful for every offer of help. It was quite emotional.

On the Wednesday, my second full day in hospital, I was told my stay would be considerably longer than I had envisaged. Results of tests so far indicated I would probably benefit best from the implant of a defibrillator. Such procedures were carried out, not in Paisley, but at The Golden Jubilee Hospital in Clydebank. I was to be transferred there whenever a bed became available.

Those operations were scheduled only for Tuesdays and Fridays. Maybe they'd squeeze me in on the Tuesday? I'd be home on the Wednesday.

CHAPTER 6: WALLS CLOSING IN.

To this point, I'd felt very positive. I hadn't dwelt on the enormity of the situation; I hadn't given any consideration as to why I should have survived; I hadn't even thought of potential ongoing ramifications. To be honest, despite the pain and discomfort, I was quite enjoying the total rest and attention.

It was like the first few novel weeks of Covid Lockdown when we were all forced to do nothing – all guilt at such inactivity was absolved. We just had to enjoy the inactivity - there was nothing we could do about it.

I'll refrain from cheap, obvious political comment.

That upbeat mood would quickly vanish on Day #3, Friday.

"Colin, we'll be moving you into one of the

communal wards later today."

No-o-o-o-o-o-o!!!!

It's crazy, I know, but I reacted worse to those words from the Staff Nurse than when I was told I'd suffered a cardiac arrest. She didn't even sedate me before breaking the news.

Now, I'm not completely anti-social. The best thing about my twenty-eight-year career in Banking was the people I worked with. And I do have some very dear friends – but these are people in whose company I choose to be.

The trouble is, our Diane asserts, I'm not very good at disguising my impatience or dislike of those I consider tiresome.

What if the guys in my room fall into that category?

OK, there's no point denying it – I should just accept the fact I'm a grumpy wee so-and-so.

 I also like my own personal space. I've been a professional dog-walker for the last sixteen years. The past couple of days had already seen my world shrink from endless miles of 'outside' and fresh air to a small, cramped private room permeated with the combined smell of disinfectant and the beef olives and cabbage being prepared for lunch.

I was mindful of some joyous people in the past telling me they thought they'd died and gone to heaven. I, on the other hand, had died and gone to Paisley.

Not that I'm complaining, you understand. Heaven can wait.

My spirit waned at an alarming rate. I knew it was all in my mind, but given it was already difficult to breathe properly because of my broken ribs, I now began to fret at the lack of fresh air.

I've never suffered from any debilitating hang-ups until just these past couple of years when I developed claustrophobic tendencies. Just two weeks prior to landing in hospital, I had to get out a friend's car as he drove us to a tennis match. I couldn't bear to be in a shared back seat. I know – it's totally irrational and I get annoyed with myself on the very odd occasion this arises.

Right now, suddenly, it was a big deal and quite troubling. I assume it manifested as a result of the trauma I'd been through a few days earlier.

It probably didn't help that reality had set in and there was no prospective discharge date being mentioned. I'd been kidding myself about how long my stay would be in hospital. I mean, it wasn't just that I'd been ill – I'd been dead! That would probably rank quite high up the table of unwellness.

It felt like the walls were closing in. Really. When I awoke in the middle of the Saturday night to find the blue curtains had been pulled around all the beds (an elderly female patient had been brought into the now spare bed in our male ward) I had to give myself a proper talking to and fight the urge to scream out.

I struggled to my feet and painful as it was, paced around what limited space I had available, taking as deep, concentrated breaths as my damaged ribs would allow.

It was like living through some weird nightmare. The two rings I'd worn on my fingers for over forty years suddenly felt constrictive. Like they were cutting off blood supply. I became panicky.

I wanted them off – **now!** It was struggle, alternatively holding them under hot and cold water in the communal toilet but eventually, I managed.

Boy, that felt so good. I'd dealt with it and managed not make a complete arse of myself. I relaxed. I was able to breathe a bit easier and managed some sleep – at least until 4am when I was rudely awakened for more blood tests.

I certainly hadn't been feeling sorry for myself. I absolutely appreciated how lucky I'd been. I knew I was receiving first class care and had been told I'd make a full recovery. I'd received way over a hundred messages on Facebook wishing me well and so many people had rallied round Diane, who'd been through such a gruelling and traumatic few days.

I took solace from the support of so many I knew were rooting for me. Yet that claustrophobic feeling of virtual imprisonment accentuated an irrational feeling of loneliness. Loneliness in the sense of not having Diane or the boys around.

In over forty years marriage, Diane and I have only spent one week apart – other than the few weekends she and the Tennis Ladies head off on a European city-break jolly.

It's funny – the three hours I'd see her each day in hospital was probably more than we'd share together at home when you factor in work commitments and my tennis / gym / running sessions. But I missed her terribly.

I have no idea where all this came from. It wasn't like me at all. But then, I don't suppose it could have been predicted how my personality would be affected following such a life-changing event.

The last thing I'd have considered though, was a cardiac arrest would turn me into a soppy old git.

*****

Some years ago, I regularly worked-out with a Physical Training Instructor for the UK Armed Forces, Special Boat Service. I recalled him saying that the mantra drummed into those soldiers being subjected to the 'beastings' of their assessment was: 'It'll soon be over.'

This wasn't the only time I'd draw upon that advice in the next couple of weeks.

CHAPTER 7:
WON A WATCH.

That first Sunday, day #5, brought good news. There were more female patients awaiting admission, and so the two of us remaining guys were to be decanted from the communal ward to the vacant private (High Dependency) rooms. I'm not so sure the other bloke was deeply overjoyed. In my mind though, I was running around the ward, waving my T-shirt above my head and knee-sliding to the heart monitor in the corner, before standing tall, arms outstretched and cockily nodding my head while sporting a smug, self-satisfied smile.

By the time Diane arrived around lunchtime, I was settled back in my old room. And … relax.

Later, as her visit was ending and she awaited a friend coming to collect her, the day just got even better – I was to be transferred to The Golden Jubilee in Clydebank. Shortly.

The ambulance was on its way!

I was excited. I'd been told how great The Jubilee was. Never-the-less, I was still a bit of a tearful mess as I said my thanks to the nurses at RAH and was wheeled out the cardiology ward in a stretcher – five leads still connecting my chest to a portable heart monitor.

I could now see some progress and was at least one step closer to getting back home.

*****

I arrived at The Golden Jubilee in Clydebank around 5pm on the Sunday. Talk about a well-oiled machine ... this was spectacular.

I was stretchered off the ambulance by the paramedics who knew to take me to Ward 2 East of the hospital. Within minutes they had me in my room (207) and transferred onto my new bed.

Two student nurses were waiting. As they began to take some basic details from me, my evening meal arrived. It was returned to a hotplate as the first of several ECGs I'd have over the coming days was recorded.

When they were finished, another lovely nurse appeared and took my blood pressure / blood sample, before yet another came to chat about my (previously non-existent) medical history and new medication / dietary requirements.

Finally, one of the doctors from the team that would be looking after me came to introduce himself. Every one of them was so warm and welcoming.

I'd been admitted only an hour previous and had been introduced to four nurses, a member of the auxiliary team and a doctor. I'd eventually also managed my evening meal which was mighty impressive for hospital food.

My room was spacious and totally private with an ensuite toilet and wet room. I even struck it lucky with a room at the back of the building, looking out over the River Clyde, along which I'd see tugs, container ships and sailing boats pass. Beyond the river were fields leading across to the small towns of Erskine and Inchinnan.

This was more like a hotel than a hospital.

I should say at this point, I think The Jubilee is the exception to the rule. Everyone knows the trouble the NHS is in, but the model adopted here seems to be a hybrid. Briefly, and from what I gleaned in conversation with the nurses, as Coronary Care specialists for the West of Scotland, The Jubilee receives funding contribution from other hospitals that 'feed' it. It was initially opened as a private venture, though the NHS subsequently bought it over. However, it retains ownership of the adjoining hotel and leisure centre which also helps fund the hospital side.

Consequently, there would appear to be a higher staff / patient ratio than elsewhere. The food also differs in that they benefit from their own in-house catering team / chefs, and not all the meals are bought in 'pre-prepared.'

(Forgive me if these basic details are not 100% correct – I've not made any great study of the circumstances … and I was on a high dosage of painkillers and other meds when I chatted about it.)

It was explained to me that I would not be having the defibrillator fitted on the coming Tuesday. There would have to be some further routine tests carried out before a definitive course of action could be prescribed. In fact, nothing would be done the following day (Monday 1st May) it being a Bank Holiday, and I should just make myself at comfortable.

Did that mean I could free myself from those infernal leads that restricted my every move?

Not a chance.

"You'll become quite attached to them by the time you leave," said one smiling, happy nurse.

I wondered how many times she'd used that line on other patients today.

*****

The following day was worry free; one to relax and enjoy my new surroundings, new routine and new company.

I'd have a visit from two of my oldest pals, Davie and Big Stevie from my athletics club. If there's one thing we could always do better than run, it was laugh. It was good to see that while our running times had naturally worsened, our ability to joke around had not diminished with age.

(There were actually **two** things we could do better than run fast and long … but I'm sure the nurses would have said something had we cracked open a few cans of beer.)

After they left, and with access to my own sink and mirror, I was able to shave my chin and head for the first time in a week. I can tell you. that felt **so** good!

Things had started to move at last –not least my bowel! I know, too much information, but that's long-stay hospital life for you, especially if prescribed Co-codamol painkillers.

*****

Before my cardiac arrest, I knew my diet was not what it should be. Although I was very fit, I was neglecting proper meals in favour of snacks – and not terribly healthy ones either. The nutrition nurse didn't hold back when I told her. So, I resolved to turn a new leaf right there and then.

I wouldn't totally expunge my diet of the rubbish I'd been eating but would drastically reduce the intake. (This was made very easy when Diane and Greig came to visit, eating all the cookies and Jelly Babies they'd brought for me.) I'd also eat all – well almost all – the fruit and veg that was provided with my meals during my stay at The Golden Jubilee.

This rather drastic lifestyle change most certainly played on my mind. The very night I made that commitment, I suffered a traumatised dream in which the nurses set me a task to complete before I could get home. I had to throw one of my beloved Empire Biscuits against a wall .... and meticulously reassemble it to its previous state before they'd sign my discharge letter!

Some might say these were mighty fine meds I was being prescribed!

*****

The first couple of mornings passed very quickly. It was a similar routine to that at the RAH, though thankfully without the 4am blood pressure check. One bonus was there were more nurses on hand, and they'd have a little bit more time for a passing chat. Everyone was so friendly.

Come the Tuesday, I convinced myself I was now over half-way through my stay. I'd be done and dusted, with the implant fitted on Friday, so only another four days till I'd be back home. I could easily manage that.

My (totally unfounded) hope was bolstered by being taken, at short notice on Wednesday for my angiogram.

The process had been outlined to me the previous

day. A dye would be passed through my bloodstream and tracked by video, the intention being to find any blocked arteries leading to that heart that may have caused my cardiac arrest. The doctors had said, given I had absolutely no warning signs of the 'event,' they didn't expect to find anything untoward, and this was just a confirmatory exercise.

I was both fascinated and impressed at how smoothly the surgical team worked. Once transferred onto the operating bed, there were immediately four nurses working on me, shortly joined by the surgeon himself.

I was conscious throughout and eased by words of encouragement from the nurses. Sedation came in the form of a shot of diazepam, and altogether it really was a bit of a dawdle – the thought of it far worse than the procedure itself.

As it happens, a narrowed artery was discovered, and a stent fired up to sort things out. This though, it was agreed, was not the root cause of what happened to me. I would have to undergo an MRI to examine the heart to ensure it was not damaged in any way. After that, a final decision would be taken on the remedial action to be taken.

Ah. Now this bit I wasn't so cool with.

CHAPTER 8:
FEARS, TEARS
& CHEERS.

It felt good being a step further down the line. Everything was starting to fall into place, though it being Thursday and still no word on when the dreaded MRI would take place, I realised the earliest I could have the implant fitted would now be the following Tuesday.

Hey ho.

At lunchtime, just as I polished off a huge helping of delicious lasagne, a nurse came to see me.

"Come on Colin, quick!" She handed me a clean bum-flasher gown and pair of paper underpants.

Never mind leaving my dignity at the hospital door, I think it had done a runner! I wondered if I'd ever see it again.

"There's been a no-show – we've got you in for your

MRI. Like, now."

Perhaps it was best I had no time to get myself worked up about this. I quickly changed and was wheeled down to the lab.

My stomach was churning. Forty minutes, I'd been told – that's how long I'd spend totally enclosed within that tight space. Still, I'd been promised I'd have some sedation that would calm my claustrophobic feelings.

"Sedation? You need sedation?" Two nurses looked at each other.

"Well ... you could have. But then you'd have to go back to your room for it to be administered and you'd miss this slot. Sorry – it's all been a bit of a rush to get you in. Do you want to go back?"

Oh dear! Well ... forget the paper pants – hand me my 'Big Boy Pants.' Time to man-up.

"No – let's just do it."

Keeping control when I wanted to scratch my arse and couldn't; remaining calm when asked to keep exhaling for longer than the ten seconds I'd primed myself for; clearing all previous claustrophobic fears from my mind .... that was one hard shift, I can tell you.

How often had I watched 'I'm A Celebrity, Get Me Out Of Here!' and shouted at the wimp of a contestant, it was simply a case of mind over matter?

Ha! Not so easy, is it Wee Man?

When it was over, I don't know if I was more relieved or chuffed with myself.

Whatever else this whole cardiac arrest recovery had in store for me, I'd be confident of handling after that.

*****

It was two days (Saturday morning) before the doctor / surgeon could have a thorough look at the MRI results. There was good news and bad news:

"The good news, Colin – there's no damage to your heart. There was that slightly narrowed artery, but we've sorted that with a stent.

"The bad news is, we can't say categorically what caused your Sudden Cardiac Arrest. After consultation with the team, it's been decided you'll benefit best from the implant of a defibrillator.

"The further bad news is this will mean you having to forfeit your driving licence to the DVLA for a period of six months."

I had primed myself for a one month driving exclusion. Six months though?! Yeah, of course I could appreciate the reasons, but this was still one heck of a shock. I am the only driver in the family; I need the car to carry out my daily work as a dog-walker.

The surgeon could see I was shattered. As

consolation, he did mention they would try to get me a slot for the operation on the following Tuesday. However, it was the king's coronation that weekend, and another Bank Holiday Monday. It could possibly be further delayed.

He said 'possibly,' but I knew he was just trying to avoid crushing my hope. He meant 'probably.'

Actually, the more I think about it, I'm sure he'd have been well versed in bedside manner. I suspect he knew he could have substituted the two words, 'could possibly' with one – 'would.'

A short while later, a nurse appeared to conduct my routine tests. She too noticed I appeared a bit down. We chatted while she took my blood pressure. When finished, she then took time to sit with me and talk about both the dogs I walk and what financial assistance may be available due to my business being affected by the driving ban.

Word soon got around, and other nurses would open chats about their dogs and pets, often spending, I suspect, a bit longer with me than was perhaps scheduled. Their professionalism and compassion were outstanding. They made me feel so at ease.

I'm sure I'm not the only patient to feel that way.

*****

I admit, I did have a bit of a wobble that evening. I'd messaged my clients to say when I was able to return to work, it would be on a bike! Consequently, there were some not-so-local dogs I would no longer be able pick up and walk. I felt a terrible sense of loss – these were my wee pals. I'd shared long, country walks with them for many years.

Alone in my room, the prospect played on my mind. For the first time in The Golden Jubilee, I felt low.

Sort yourself out, man!

I ate some Jelly Babies. Actually, I ate a lot of Jelly Babies.

All was right with the world again.

The rest of the holiday weekend was fine. There was plenty football to watch on my laptop. This countered the wall-to-wall general TV coverage of The Coronation, which was not really my bag.

Tuesday dawned. I was placed on 'nil by mouth' fast. (This was in addition to the 'nil by jokes – he has sore ribs' hand-written instruction left by my athletics club pals.) Nothing to eat or drink from midnight on the Monday. I was to have my defibrillator fitted at last. Once again, I had to don the unflattering but completely flappable gown. Yes – and the baggy paper undies.

I spent the morning and early afternoon kicking my heels, unable to concentrate on anything. Even Loose Women drifted over my head. When a nurse appeared at my door, I was simultaneously filled with excitement and dread. Let's do this!

"Colin, I'm sorry. I have some bad news I'm afraid," she said rather sheepishly.

I knew what was coming.

"We're having to postpone your operation today. There's been an emergency admission."

The poor young nurse. I could see she was dreading my reaction. Obviously, I was gutted, not to mention starving, but there's little to be achieved in being annoyed with someone doing their best to save your life.

"Don't worry," I said. "I was 'an emergency' myself last week. I understand."

I meant it. I was out of immediate danger now and was being monitored 24/7. I really felt for the newly admitted patient and their family.

Oh well – on the upside, 'A Place in the Sun' would soon be on TV. And it was rhubarb crumble and custard for lunchtime dessert, if I wasn't too late.

*****

Later that evening my patience and understanding brought reward - the hospital had arranged an extra surgical slot for the following day, and I would be having my procedure. Definitely. All being well, I'd be allowed home on the Thursday.

True to their word, I was whisked down to the lab around lunchtime on Wednesday.

I'd not been concerned about the operation at all, but

as the time drew near, I grew a little anxious. The thought of lying awake while a surgeon opened me up below my left collar bone and not only inserted a small battery-powered box under my skin, but connected two leads into my heart, wasn't one I relished.

I think I'd probably watched too many gory TV documentaries on surgical procedures for my own good.

I needn't have worried. The anaesthetist herself and another nurse collected me from my room and parked me up in the operating room. As with the angiogram procedure, a team of doctors and nurses swiftly mobilised with military precision, prepping me while the surgeon and his assistants outlined what would be happening over the next forty minutes or so.

It was all done in such a relaxed manner, the surgeons cracking a few jokes and winding me up; the anaesthetist and others on her side of the operating table casually taking about gardening.

I was given some gas and air type sedation and a local anaesthetic, the latter being administered so expertly, I swear I didn't even feel the 'scratch' of the needle piercing my skin. I was asked to look to my right while the work was being done on my left side. A large blue tarpaulin type cover was loosely placed over me, so there was little chance of me seeing what was going on – not that I particularly wanted to.

I could feel some pushing and pulling as the surgeon inserted the device and connected it up. Thankfully, I didn't hear any mumbled swearing, so my confidence in his ability remained high.

And then it was done. I was invited down from the operating table and to walk over to my bed which was then pushed back to my room.

As I passed the nurses hub / reception area, several of those who had been caring for me, smiled, waved and quickly asked how I felt. It's silly, but little things like that made my whole stay pleasurable in a strange kind of way.

Back in my room, I was told I'd have to remain in bed until the next morning – eighteen hours away. I was still benefitting the effects of the painkiller and sedation and felt totally fine, but I'd do as I was told.

Throughout the afternoon and evening, I continued to feel great. This was easy. Then, around one in the morning, the meds wore off. Bang! The next few hours were a tad uncomfortable, I have to say.

*****

Thursday morning was a bit different to others. I had my device tested; all good. I had an X-Ray to check the leads into my heart had not shifted position; all good. One of the surgeons called round to check how I was and answer any remaining questions I had; all good. Finally, one of my regular nurses went through all the medication I'd be taking home with me; all good again – though the number of tablets I'd be on, at least initially, was a bit disconcerting considering all I'd ever taken before was paracetamol and the very occasional anti-biotic.

Time dragged till my discharge. It was a weird period of limbo. Strangely, as much as I was excited to be going home, I was also a little bit sad.

My regular nurse of the previous few days asked if she'd push me in a wheelchair to the Discharge Room to await collection by Diane and our friend, Anne.

Walking a bit more than a hundred metres did seem a little daunting, considering I'd been restricted to only ten or so at a time for over a fortnight. But no thanks. Defiant, proud and I confess, a little bit vain, I wanted to make it under my own steam.

As I passed the nurses hub / reception desk, a couple other nurses called out.

"Yeah – Colin's going home today," replied my accompanying nurse. Turning towards me, she added quietly, "You're going to be missed in here, you know."

That was it … tears instantly welled in my eyes. Here we go again!

I'm sure the nursing staff are used to this kind of reaction – I defy anyone who has been in their care for any length of time not to be similarly affected.

My ward nurse got me settled into a chair in the large, empty waiting room and handed me over to the Discharge Nurse.

"Bye Colin. Good luck in your recovery. Behave yourself."

And she was gone.

Silence.

I looked around the empty room. I was happy. Very happy and positive. I'd been through a lot and come out the other side. There was still some way to go, of course but I couldn't wait to get started.

Yet there was a bit of me felt guilty in that I could never thank the staff at The Golden Jubilee enough.

CHAPTER 9: HOME.

By the time Anne had dropped Diane and myself back at our house, I'd been away from home longer than I'd normally be on vacation. Sixteen days on holiday would have felt refreshing; sixteen days in hospital cannot, despite the care and attention received, be termed 'restful.' The early morning medical tests; the discomfort in sleeping; the boredom; the sheer restrictiveness, and lack of beer are not the kind of terms you'd readily use on a postcard from sunnier climes.

I still registered that familiar feeling of change as we drove into the village. The trees and shrubs were now in full leaf; the fields had turned verdant; the birdsong had changed, heralding warmer times ahead.

Diane dropped my collection of hospital clothes, books and toiletries in the house, and we sat in the garden, warmed by the last rays of sunshine before they disappeared behind the now bushy branches of the trees in the woods behind us.

For over two weeks, I'd been gasping for a beer. Now though, a strong coffee just seemed more appropriate. My two cats, Suki and Lulu appeared.

"Oh you're back. Good to see you."

They rubbed up against my leg, waited to have their ears scratched, then promptly buggered off again.

Some things change; some don't.

CHAPTER 10: GETTING EMOTIONAL.

I know, from reading posts on various social media sites, that many people who have experienced a similar personal trauma, have subsequently suffered from bursting into floods of tears without warning.

I wouldn't consider myself a terribly emotional guy, and so far, I've not had any issues with this at all. I'm happy to talk about my experience (heck – I'm writing this nonsense for a start) and perhaps the focus of this, and the subsequent attention I've been afforded has been so diversionary, it's simply cathartic.

I've had my moments though. Not so much in an introspective 'why me?' / 'why did I survive' kind of way, but more in relating the simple acts of kindness and care I've received.

Saying 'goodbye' to the nurses in both the RAH and Golden Jubilee hospitals was tricky. Especially so in the case of the latter as I'd spent over twice as long there and had got to know them all more. I dreaded that moment of handing over a few boxes of chocolates and a Thank You card.

(I know, it seems so insignificant, but I lacked any better inspiration.)

Then there were the times at The Golden Jubilee when I was asked bout how I came to be admitted to hospital in the first place. I really choked back tears as I related the set of coincidences that led to me being alive. The reaction of the nurses – rubbing my arm and offering positive words of comfort – had me in bits.

The only other time I struggled was when telling Diane of the reaction from my football club. It had been a great season for Renfrew FC. In my thirty-three years, we have won the Scottish Cup, and a couple other trophies, but never have we scored a League and Cup double.

The manager took time out to message me and ask if I'd make it to final game of the season and the presentation of the League Trophy. If not, he offered to come to my home so I could have photos taken.

As it happens, I did get along to that game, courtesy of fellow fan and friend, Alan who drove me to and from the ground. To be welcomed back by so many people, friends and other supporters, players, management and committee, and to have an announcement made over the tannoy system at half time was quite overwhelming.

*****

Surprisingly, the time I was sure I'd be an emotional wreck, was the one occasion I totally held it together.

Within a day or so of being admitted to hospital and thanks to some detective work on social media by my younger son Brett, I was able to contact the two policemen who saved my life. We agreed to meet up shortly after I was allowed home.

On the Sunday, three days after being discharged, PCs Kyle Reid and Aidan Jenner dropped by. They were on a break from their late afternoon shift and spent about twenty minutes in our home, during which we chatted about the events surrounding my cardiac arrest and our common interest in local football.

Though it was the first time we'd met (well, the first I remembered at least) it was like chatting to two old friends. Conversation was not stilted or awkward in the slightest. They were just genuinely delighted to see I was alive and recovering so well; Diane and I were so happy we were able to meet and thank them in person.

CHAPTER 11: A PERFECT ALIGNMENT.

I've read that of all people who suffer an 'out of hospital' cardiac arrest, only eight percent survive. Through discussion with the doctors and surgeons coupled with our subsequent meeting and chat with PCs Reid and Jenner, it became even more apparent just how lucky I had been to survive my cardiac arrest.

The set of coincidental circumstances that led to me being here today is quite extraordinary. Had any one of the following not occurred, then I would either have been alone when I suffered the massive heart failure, or I'd have been driving through heavy rush-hour traffic.

1) Diane normally doesn't need me to pick her up from work.

2) I decided to go a run before collecting Diane,

which meant I approached our meeting point from a different direction and so collected her from within the car park.

3) As the incident unfolded, Diane was so quick in trying to pull me from the car and attract the attention of the police.

4) The two policemen, Kyle and Aidan, were only in the car park so Kyle could buy some food from Tesco for his evening shift snack.

5) While in Tesco, Kyle met a friend and they briefly chatted - otherwise, he'd have re-joined Aidan minutes earlier and been back out on patrol.

6) Aidan had only just completed his CPR training the week before.

7) Kyle realised the nearby, large Tesco store would have a public use defibrillator readily available and was quick to retrieve it.

8) The equally wonderful paramedics were deployed from the local ambulance station in Linwood (about a mile away) and were on hand within five minutes of the call being placed.

9) Paisley's RAH hospital (to where I was initially admitted) is also only a 5 minute, 'blue light' drive away.

10) Had I not been so fit, it would have been unlikely I'd have survived. (I may not have ever won a world class medal, but more than any Olympic athlete, it seems I'd been training my whole life for this one

moment.)

Poor Aidan – just days previous he was practicing CPR on a dummy. Now he was doing it for real ... yeah, I know – on another dummy! This time though, one with ribs, which he heard crack and break as he performed the life-saving action. Keeping calm and professional in such trying and traumatic circumstances, especially so early in his career, is truly commendable.

All in all, I am one very lucky dude. Someone or something was working in my favour that evening for everything to align as they did.

But more than 'luck,' I owe so much to the amazing professionalism of two local policemen.

My family and I can never thank them enough.

CHAPTER 12:
MEDIA INTEREST.

I don't think I'm one to normally dwell too much on the past – unless I've played poorly in a tennis match. Then I really beat myself up for a couple of days. Goodness knows why, it's not like I'm much bloody good anyway!

Since being allowed home, I've not spent much time considering on the whys and wherefores of what happened. This has been aided in no small part by the distraction created initially by social media, which led to local and even national mainstream media coverage.

You know, I'm quite obviously neither media-savvy, nor a youngster able to generate an income from becoming an 'influencer' on You Tube or whatever. Rather, I've spent years trying to gain a wider interest in a couple of blogs I run, and the two little books I've previously written.

Little did I realise all I had to do was suffer a cardiac

arrest and post a picture on Facebook of me with the two young men who saved my life.

Granted the photo was quite striking. I am five feet, four inches short. In the picture, I'm standing between two policemen each over a foot taller. I look about twelve years old, not sixty-four.

Maybe it was the almost comical nature of the photo, or perhaps just the simple 'good news' story that it reflected. Whatever, once posted to my Facebook page, it was shared numerous times and ended up going viral. It was re-posted by friends and family of the two policemen; shared on a couple of internal Police pages and on Twitter.

The number of hits it received attracted the interest of local press, and the following day I had phone calls from two local papers and one from Glasgow city, all of whom wanted to have a chat about what happened and send round photographers.

The story was big news over the next week and not only in the written press. Ex Scotland rugby player John Beattie phoned and an hour or so later, I was relating my story on national BBC Radio Scotland's popular Drivetime Show.

A week later, and there was still some Press interest though this time we were no longer on the front page but relegated to page 11 of another local paper. I did see the article again later in the week, but this time it was tightly wrapped around a steaming bundle of fish 'n' chips.

Fame can be so cruelly fickle.

CHAPTER 13: SMELL THE COFFEE & LAUGH.

On leaving hospital, I was told to do nothing for a couple of weeks at least. I wasn't to know then, but there appears to be two different definitions of the word 'nothing.' There's what generally active people like me call 'nothing,' and then there's the hospital interpretation of the word. The latter means 'absolutely nothing;' nada; zip, 'hee-haw;' sweet F.A.' It doesn't mean washing dishes, sorting ironing, emptying bins or even just watching your tennis team play a match.

Of course, I realise that now, but it took three very uncomfortable and sore days for the penny to drop. On reflection, a cardiac arrest is rather serious, and I should have realised my body, while it felt good and strong, had been through a bit of a traumatic event.

Poor Diane – she won't let me do anything now and

is having to cope with everything around the house and garden.

Total rest does work though and a week or so later I was feeling much better.

*****

When I set about writing this short-read record of my experience, I made the conscious decision to keep it light. While I appreciate not everyone who goes through a similar experience will deal with it in similar fashion, it is a genuine reflection of how I've coped with the whole affair.

Us Glaswegians are often regarded as 'glass half-full' people. We do like a good old moan; there's little point denying. However, somewhat surprisingly, I've found myself very much not even 'glass half **full**' but **three quarters** full when it comes to looking ahead this time.

I genuinely feel excited by what lies ahead.

I take the view that now I've had a stent fitted, there is a lesser chance of suffering a similar event – though obviously there are various reasons why it **could** happen again.

However, as a back-up measure to that possibility I've also had an ICD (Implantable Cardioverter Defibrillator) fitted. Should I again suffer a cardiac arrest, for whatever reason, I have the safety net of the implant kicking in and keeping me alive.

I could fear for the future; I'd be a liar to say I've not considered the worst-case scenario, but really, worrying over something that may never happen will help neither me nor my family and friends.

Life will never be quite the same again. Wouldn't it be so boring if it was? Changes will have to be made, but I'll embrace that.

I'll embrace my new body image. I'd like to think the implant will give the impression I have been doing some extra gym-work on my pecs. In truth though, when covered by a tight-fitting T-shirt, it looks like I'm carrying a ten-pack of Benson & Hedges in my breast pocket.

It will be my badge of honour though – a conversation starter.

I'll change my diet for the better, though I can't promise to cut out the Empire Biscuits entirely; I'll wear my 'good clothes' more often and listen to my special records more regularly. I'll tell Diane, Greig, Brett and the rest of my family more frequently just how much I love them.

OK – I can't drive for at least six months from the date my ICD was installed. That's not going to be much fun, especially as I'm the only driver in the household. Yet there are some plus-points to this:

- I don't need to set time aside to go do the weekly shopping; it's all done online now.
- I don't have to worry if the heap of rust is going to start every morning.

- I don't have to wash it every single week.
- I save on petrol cost, and I qualify for a free bus-pass, so I'm 'quids-in.'
- I also save on inevitable repair costs to a ten-year-old car with 125,000 miles on the clock.
- The car has an effective extended shelf-life of six months.
- I can drink beer whenever I want – I don't have to count alcohol units and work forward to the time I can safely drive again.

Again, on the up-side, I've been told I **will** be able to return to my sporting interests. This however may come as a disappointment to my tennis partners who would have been excited at the thought of being able to drop me without any awkward conversation.

I have though promised Diane that I will no longer push myself to compete with those younger than me at Circuit Training; that I'll stop continuously looking to better my times over one / two / three-mile runs; that I won't try for a sub-22-minute PB over 5K on my forthcoming sixty-fifth birthday.

I will from now on, run simply to keep generally fit. I'm sure that in the not to distant future an acceptance will come that at my age, it would become physically impossible to keep going faster anyway.

I'm very happy now, that rather than being

remembered as 'the fittest guy I knew' it's better to be **known** as 'the guy who used to be so fit,' by friends and family.

To say I've been given a 'second chance' would perhaps imply I messed up on the first one. I'm not so sure about that – I think I've done OK up till now. No, what's possibly happened is my 'pause button' has been pressed, affording me time to savour times past and assess my forward path.

My hope is to continue along that very same path for many years to come. Maybe I'll ease back, take my time and appreciate more of what's going on around me. Smell the coffee and all that.

Yeah – 'appreciate.' That's key. Appreciate who and what I have; appreciate my surroundings; appreciate my friends and family; appreciate this reflective time; appreciate just how lucky I am in so many respects.

I already appreciate what happened to me on 23rd April 2023 was a bit of an unfortunate accident and I've accepted the profuse apologies of Life, Death and Fate for the inconvenience they inadvertently caused.

What it highlighted though, is we never know the minute. Every day is precious. We should not be wasteful of time.

It was Charlie Chaplin who once famously said:

'A day without laughter is a day wasted.'

Of course, a Sudden Cardiac Arrest is no laughing matter, but then again, you know what they say is the 'best medicine.'

Me? I'm leaving nothing to chance. Although I have a raft of meds to help prevent a repeat episode, I'm going with wee Charlie on this one. Whether it's medically proven or not, I figure it doesn't hurt to laugh – well it does right now because of my broken ribs, but you know what I mean.

I don't plan on wasting one single day.

I'm going to laugh. A lot.

I hope you can too.

THE END

CEE TEE JACKSON

FOREVER IN THEIR DEBT.

*PC AIDAN JENNER &
PC KYLE REID.*

ABOUT THE AUTHOR

Colin (Cee Tee) Jackson

Cee Tee (Colin) Jackson is a Petcare Professional / Dog Walker of sixteen years' experience, having previously spent twenty-eight years in UK Branch Banking.

A short-arse with an even shorter attention span, he has written two books prior to this – both on the short side also.

He is a keen music enthusiast with a large record collection and some years ago wrote for the UK magazine, Artrocker. Nowadays, he concentrates more on blogging; one covering general memories of the 1970s, the other focussing on the more niche subject of obscure bands from the 1960s and '70s.

Colin's spare time revolves around sport: football

(now just watching); tennis (playing, though not very well); gym /circuit training and running. He has also competed at baseball in both English and Scottish leagues.

Married to Diane for over forty years, they have two grown sons, Greig and Brett and share their home with two rescued, feral cats, Suki & Lulu.

*****

COLIN'S BLOGS:

ceeteejackson.com - an author and his nonsense

onceuponatimeinthe70s.com - shared tales of growing up and living through the late 1960s & '70s

loudhorizon.com - underplayed underground music from the '60s & '70s

BOOKS BY THIS AUTHOR

Damp Dogs & Rabbit Wee

Cast off; ripped off; cheesed off.When redundancy strikes for the second time in two years, an ex-bank manager is thrust into the world of the self-employed through a desire to eat and meet his mortgage payments.

A series of animal-related vignettes, present an amusing, charming and compassionate look at the life of a Pet Professional. (OK - I'm a dog walker.)

From the scary to the farcical; the tender to the messy and the cute to the psychopaths - you've got to laugh. Smile, at least.Proving there's more to dog walking than simply walking dogs, DAMP DOGS & RABBIT WEE is a humorous, light read that will appeal to all pet owners, animal lovers and yes, dog walkers.

Give The Dog A Home

Goa, India's smallest state, has much to offer: a tropical climate; long, golden beaches fringed by coconut trees; wonderful food; friendly, happy and welcoming people – and dogs.

Lots of dogs.

Through gently humorous observation and heart-warming tales of love and devotion, GIVE THE DOG A HOME gives a brief insight into the life of Goa's homeless beach and street dogs.

Printed in Great Britain
by Amazon

23562903R00046